Poems of a widow

Poems of a widow

collection of Poms created
by a widow

The pangs of dispare grief do sting,
Like a thousand daggers, sharp and bright.
It pierces deep, and cuts like a ring,
Leaving scars that will not soon take flight.

The weight of sorrow, a crushing load,
That presses down, and makes one feel so low.
The tears that flow, a never-ending tide,
A grief so deep, it cannot subside.

The memories of what could have been,
Haunt every moment, every scene.
The what-ifs and the maybes, a refrain,
Echoing through the chambers of the brain.

But still we hold on, to hope's thin thread,
And pray that someday, grief will be dead.
For in its place, a brighter day will shine,

And   love   will   conquer,   and   all   will   be   divine.

In twilight's hush, where shadows dance and play,
I weep for thee, my love, lost yesterday.
The world may see me smile, but they can't hear
The whispers of my heart, its deepest fear.

The stars above, they twinkle with a tear,
As if they knew our love, so pure and clear.
The wind it whispers secrets of the night,
Of memories we shared, so bright and light.

The moon it glows with gentle grace,
A beacon in the darkness of my place.
For in its light, I see thy face so fair,
And know that thou art gone, beyond compare.

The waves they crash upon the shore,
A symphony of sorrow, evermore.
Their melody a reminder of thy embrace,
And how thy love, it left its trace.

The trees they sway, a funeral dirge,
A mournful sound, that pierces my nurse.
Their leaves they rustle, a sorrowful refrain,
A reminder of the love we gained.
In the quiet of the night, I weep
For a love lost, a soul adrift
Grief wraps around my heart like a shroud
And despair hangs heavy in the air

Memories of laughter and tender touch
Now haunt my every waking moment
The warmth of love turned cold and distant

Leaving me lost in a sea of sorrow

The echoes of your voice still linger
A cruel reminder of what once was
But now, only silence fills the void
And the ache of longing consumes me

I search for solace in the depths of darkness
Hoping to find a glimmer of hope
But all I find is the emptiness of a love
That slipped through my trembling fingers

So I carry the weight of love lost
And the burden of grief and despair
As I navigate this unfamiliar terrain
Yearning for the light that once guided me

Trapt in darkness, I feel the weight
Of the shadows closing in around me
No light to guide my weary soul
Just the suffocating embrace of night

The darkness whispers cruel secrets
And I am lost in its tangled web
A prisoner of my own despair
Yearning for a glimpse of dawn

In the depths of this endless night
I search for a glimmer of hope
But the darkness holds me tightly
Refusing to release its hold

I long to break free from this abyss
To find the warmth of the sun's embrace
But for now, I am trapt in darkness
Aching for the light to set me free

Sadness holds me like an anchor
Weighted and unyielding
Dragging me deeper into the abyss
Where light struggles to penetrate

The heaviness settles in my chest
A constant ache that never fades
It wraps around me like a suffocating shroud
Leaving me gasping for air

I try to shake it off, to break free
But it clings to me like a relentless shadow
Whispering doubts and fears in my ear
A constant companion in my solitude

I long to be released from its grasp
To feel lightness and joy once more
But for now, sadness holds me tight
And I am enveloped in its embrace

Hold on, don't give up
When the storm rages on
And the darkness threatens to consume
Remember, the sun will rise again

In the depths of despair
Where hope seems but a distant memory
Hold on, don't give up
For even the smallest flame can pierce the night

The weight of the world may bear down
Crushing spirits and dreams alike
But hold on, don't give up
For strength lies in the unyielding heart

When the road ahead seems endless
And the journey filled with endless trials
Hold on, don't give up
For victory awaits the relentless soul

So let the echoes of doubt fade away
And embrace the resilience within
Hold on, don't give up
For the dawn of triumph is but a breath away
In the stillness of the morning,
I close my eyes and envision
the life I long to create,
manifesting my dreams into reality.

I feel the warmth of the sun
as it touches my skin,
and I breathe in the possibilities
that the universe has to offer.

With each step I take,
I am guided by the power within,
manifesting abundance and joy
in every corner of my existence.

As I open my heart to the world,
I embrace the magic of manifesting,
knowing that my desires are already
taking shape in the tapestry of life.

In the quiet stillness of dawn,
I paint my dreams with golden hues,
Manifesting my dream life,
In the whispers of morning light.

I breathe in possibility,
Each exhale a step closer,
To the life I've always envisioned,
Manifesting my dream life.

With each heartbeat, I build,
A world of abundance and joy,
Where my passions ignite,
And my soul dances freely.

I am the architect of my destiny,
With every thought and action,
I am manifesting my dream life,
Into a beautiful reality.

In the depth of darkness, I searched for a glimmer
A spark to ignite the shadows within
Lost in the labyrinth of despair and doubt
I yearned for the warmth of the sun's embrace

Through the silence, a whisper of hope
A faint flicker in the vast expanse
Guiding me through the endless night
Leading me towards the dawn's gentle touch

As I emerged from the shroud of gloom
I felt the weight of sorrow lift from my shoulders
The colors of life danced before my eyes
And I found solace in the embrace of the light

Now I bask in the radiance of a new day
A testament to the resilience of the human spirit
For in the darkest moments, I discovered
The beauty of finding the light after darkness.

The morning chaos, the endless demands
Of little voices and tiny hands
The constant juggle, the never-ending race
Sometimes it feels like I'm losing the pace

The dishes pile up, the laundry overflows
The tantrums and tears, the never-ending woes
I long for a moment of peace and quiet
But it seems like an impossible, distant sight

The weight of responsibility, the never-ending to-dos
The guilt of not being enough, the never-ending blues
I love them more than words can say
But sometimes, I just need a break in the fray

But amidst the chaos, there's love and joy
Tiny hugs and laughter that I can't destroy
I may be frustrated, but I wouldn't trade
This beautiful, messy mumlife that I've made

In the darkness of night
A glimmer of light
A whisper of possibility
Hope blooms in the heart

Like a seed in the soil
It pushes through the cracks
Seeking the warmth of the sun
And the promise of tomorrow

In the stillness of the night
I search for your presence
But find only echoes of your laughter
Fading into the silence

Memories linger like shadows
Haunting every corner of my heart
A love once vibrant, now lost
Leaving me adrift in a sea of longing

Alone in the night, the silence echoes
No longer a partner to share the day
Memories linger, whispers in the dark
A heart heavy with the weight of loss

Empty spaces once filled with laughter
Now echo with the absence of your touch
The world moves on, but I am frozen
A widow left to navigate this life alone

Alone in the night, I find solace in memories
Of the love that once filled this empty space
His laughter still echoes in the silent rooms
But now it's only the shadows that embrace

The warmth of his touch still lingers on my skin
A bittersweet reminder of what I've lost
His absence a heavy weight on my weary shoulders
As I navigate this unfamiliar path alone

The world moves on, but I am frozen in time
A widow's veil shrouds my grieving heart
I long to hear his voice, to feel his presence
But all that remains are echoes of the past

Yet in the stillness, I find moments of peace
In the quietude of our once-shared domain
I am a widow, but I am also a survivor
Learning to embrace the love that still remains

Will I find love again being a widow
The ache in my heart seems too heavy to bear
Memories of laughter and warmth still linger
But the future feels empty, devoid of care

The touch of his hand, the sound of his voice
Haunts me in the quiet moments of the night
I long for companionship, for a love that's true
But fear it's impossible, an unattainable sight

Grief and longing intertwine within my soul
Yearning for a connection, a new beginning
But the fear of loss looms over my heart
Will I find love again, or forever be mourning?

The silence of the empty room
Echoes the loneliness in her heart
The warmth of his presence
Gone with the setting sun

Memories linger in the air
His laughter, her solace
Now just a distant whisper
Lost in the void of solitude

The days stretch out endlessly
No hand to hold, no one to share
She longs for his comforting embrace
But he's forever beyond her reach

The world moves on, but she's frozen
In the solitude of her widow's sorrow
Aching for the love that once filled her days
Alone in the quiet, she carries on

In the gentle embrace of motherhood's love,
A symphony of tenderness and grace,
A melody that echoes from above,
A lullaby that cradles every trace.

Her arms, a haven of warmth and solace,
Her voice, a soothing serenade of peace,
Her love, a gift that never knows malice,
Her touch, a balm that makes all worries cease.

With every heartbeat, she sings a refrain,
Of sacrifice, of joy, of endless care,
Her love, a sonnet without a single stain,
A ballad that weaves through every whispered prayer.

In the dance of motherhood's sweet embrace,
Love's melody weaves through time and space.

In the garden of life, we plant our dreams
Seeds of hope, buried in the fertile soil
Nurtured by the sun's warm embrace
Slowly, steadily, they begin to grow

Tiny shoots emerge, reaching for the sky
Tender leaves unfurl, dancing in the breeze
Roots delve deep, anchoring in the earth
A testament to the beauty of growth

In a world of wonders, where dreams come true,
Where the ordinary becomes something new.
There lies a realm, filled with enchantment and charm,
A place where magic weaves its spell, calm and warm.

In this land of mystique, where imagination soars,
Where the impossible opens infinite doors.
Whispers of spells and potions fill the air,
As stars twinkle above, with a magical flair.

With a wave of a wand, and a flick of a wrist,
A magician creates moments impossible to resist.
Rabbits appear from hats, cards dance in the air,
As the audience gasps, caught in the spell's snare.

Fairies flutter and sprinkle pixie dust,
Granting wishes and turning dreams to must.
Unicorns gallop, with grace and noble pride,
Their magical presence, impossible to hide

In the depths of the forest, where secrets lie,
Creatures of myth and legend catch the eye.
Dragons breathe fire, lighting up the night,
While mermaids sing melodies, pure and bright.

Oh, the wonders of magic, so captivating and grand,
A realm where miracles are held in the palm of your hand.
Believe in the power, let your imagination unfurl,
For in this world of magic, dreams become a whirl.

So let your heart embrace the mystical and the unknown,
Let the magic within you forever be shown.
For in this realm of wonders, where dreams come true,
Magic lives on, and it lives within you.

Sparkling Stardust

In the midnight sky, a sprinkle of stardust falls,
Unveiling a world where magic enthralls.
Whispers of secrets, in the moonlight's glow,
Where dreams take flight, and wonders grow.

Wand's Delight

With a wave of a wand, dreams ignite,
Sparks of magic, shining bright.
In whispered incantations, spells unfold,
Unleashing enchantment, untold.

Fairy's Dance

In a hidden grove, where moonbeams play,
Fairies twirl in a magical ballet.
Their wings aglow with ethereal light,
A dance of wonder, in the hushed night.

Spellbound Whispers

In ancient tomes, secrets reside,
In whispered words, magic's guide.
Spells whispered softly, with utmost care,
Unlocking realms where dreams dare.

Enchanted Embrace

In nature's embrace, magic weaves,
Through whispering leaves and rustling trees.
The wind, a spell, caresses the air,
A world enchanted, beyond compare.

In a realm where dreams come alive,
Where wonder and enchantment thrive,
There lies a realm of mystic hue,
Where magic weaves its spell anew.

With a flicker of a wand, a whispered word,
A world of possibilities is stirred.
Through ancient incantations and secret lore,
A symphony of spells, forevermore.

From sparkling stars that light the night,
To potions brewed with lunar light,
The power of the arcane, so pure and grand,
Guides us through a whimsical wonderland.

Through hidden forests, where fairies roam,
Their wings aflutter, as they call this home.
With a touch of their magic, they make us see,
The beauty in every leaf, every tree.

In the realm of magic, dreams take flight,
Where wizards soar on broomsticks, in the night.
With their wands held high, they cast their spells,
Creating wonders that no one can foretell.

But magic, dear friend, is not just a show,
It's a spark within us, waiting to glow.
Believe in the power that lies within,
And let the magic of life truly begin.

So let your spirit dance, embrace the unknown,
For in the realm of magic, you're not alone.
Open your heart, let your imagination soar,
And you'll find that magic is forevermore.

Trapped in the labyrinth of your mind,
A place where thoughts and emotions intertwine.
A maze of memories, hopes, and fears,
A world of doubts and unshed tears.

In this mental prison, you're confined,
Lost in the corridors of your own design.
The walls are high, the doors are locked,
Escape seems impossible, all pathways blocked.

Each thought is a twist, each feeling a turn,
As you wander through the thoughts that churn.
The echoes of past mistakes haunt your way,
Creating a darkness that's hard to sway.

But within this maze, there's a glimmer of light,
A flicker of hope shining ever so bright.
For the mind is a powerful force indeed,
With the strength to heal and to succeed.

Unlock the doors, break down the walls,
Embrace the freedom that your spirit calls.
Challenge the doubts, release the chains,
Allow your thoughts to flow like gentle rains.

Find solace in the beauty of your own mind,
Discover the treasures you're destined to find.
Embrace the journey, both rough and kind,
And let your spirit soar, leaving the past behind.

For within your mind lies endless possibility,
A universe waiting to be explored with curiosity.
Don't let the maze keep you confined,
Break free, and let your true essence shine.

Love and grief, intertwined in a dance,
A bittersweet symphony, a lifelong romance.
For love, a tender flame that warms the heart,
But grief, a stormy sea that tears apart.

Love, a gentle touch, a whispered word,
A feeling so profound, it's never absurd.
But grief, a heavy weight, a silent cry,
A pain so deep, it makes one wonder why.

Love, a blooming flower, full of grace,
A connection so pure, it cannot be replaced.
But grief, a withering leaf, fading away,
Leaving behind emptiness, day by day.

Love, a bright star, guiding the way,
A beacon of hope, even in the gray.
But grief, a dark cloud, blocking the sun,
Casting shadows, until the day is done.

Love and grief, a paradoxical pair,
Both necessary, in this world we share.
For love teaches us to cherish and adore,
While grief reminds us of what's worth fighting for.

My Little Stars

In the vast sky of my life, they shine so bright,
My children, my little stars, my guiding light.
Each one unique, with their own special glow,
They fill my heart with love, a joy I'll always know.

Their laughter, like twinkling constellations above,
Brings warmth and happiness, a mother's purest love.
Their smiles, like the sun breaking through the clouds,
Illuminate my days, like nature's miracles allowed.

In their eyes, I see a world full of dreams,
A future of endless possibilities, it seems.
With every step they take, my heart soars high,
For my children, my little stars, make me reach the sky.

A Mother's Song

In the melody of life, my children are the notes,
A symphony of love, the sweetest antidote.
Their laughter, like music, fills my soul,
A song of joy that makes me whole.

With each passing day, they grow and learn,
In their innocence, my heart begins to yearn.
To protect and guide them, a mother's sacred duty,
To nurture their dreams, and let their spirits fly free.

Their smiles, like melodies, brighten up my days,
Their hugs, like harmonies, bring warmth always.
In this song of motherhood, their voices ring true,
For my children, my precious notes, my love forever grew.

Footprints in My Heart

Tiny feet, leaving footprints on my heart,
My children, my treasures, a work of art.
With every step they take, my love expands,
For they are the ones who truly understand.

Their laughter, like music, fills the air,
A sweet melody, beyond compare.
Their tears, like raindrops, cleanse my soul,
For in their happiness, I find my role.

Their dreams, like whispers, inspire my days,
Their hugs, like embraces, light up my ways.
In the journey of motherhood, we walk hand in hand,
For my children, my footprints, forever will stand.

Unconditional Love

In a world of fleeting emotions and changing tides,
My children, my anchors, in whom my heart confides.
Their love, pure and unconditional, knows no bounds,
A treasure so precious, forever it surrounds.

Through sleepless nights and endless days,
Their presence gives me strength, in so many ways.
Their smiles, like sunshine, brighten up my soul,
Their love, like a warm embrace, makes me whole.

In their laughter, I find joy beyond compare,
In their tears, I find empathy and care.
For my children, my forever loves, I'll always be near,
With a love that's unwavering, sincere, and clear.

Growing Together

From tiny hands to outstretched arms,
My children, my blessings, a world of charms.
Together we grow, through the ups and downs,
A bond so strong, it knows no bounds.

Their first steps, a milestone of pride,
Their first words, a symphony to guide.
In their triumphs, I find strength and delight,
In their struggles, I find the will to fight.

Through every stage, we learn and explore,
Together we laugh, cry, and soar.
For my children, my companions, my loves so true,
I am forever grateful for the journey with you.

Embracing Failure

Failure, my dear friend, come take my hand,
For in your presence, I understand.
You are not my enemy, but a gentle guide,
Leading me on a path where growth resides.

Through your lessons, I learn to persevere,
To rise above the doubts and conquer fear.
You teach me humility, to accept my flaws,
And find strength in the face of life's applause.

In your embrace, I find the courage to try,
To push beyond limits and reach for the sky.
For failure is not the end, but a stepping stone,
To build resilience and make success my own.

Lessons in Failure

Failure, a teacher dressed in disguise,
Unveiling wisdom hidden behind our tries.
In every stumble and fall, a lesson unfolds,
A chance to learn, to grow, and to behold.

It is through failure, we find our way,
To navigate the darkness and see the ray.
For success is not defined by the absence of mistakes,
But by the resilience to rise when courage shakes.

So let failure be our guide, our compass true,
To lead us to the dreams we once thought few.
For in the face of failure, we find our strength,
And realize that failure is not the end, but a journey's length.

Failing Forward

Failure, a stepping stone on the path we tread,
A reminder that success is not easily fed.
With each stumble and setback, we gain insight,
To push through the darkness and embrace the light.

For failure is not a mark of defeat,
But an opportunity to rise and repeat.
To learn from our mistakes, to evolve and grow,
And let resilience and determination show.

So let us embrace failure with open arms,
For it is through failure, we unlock our charms.
To fail forward, and never be afraid,
For failure is but a step towards the life we've made.

The Beauty of Failure

Failure, an artist with a unique touch,
Creating masterpieces from life's smudge.
In every broken dream and shattered plan,
A canvas for resilience to take a stand.

For failure paints the colors of our soul,
The shades of strength that make us whole.
It teaches us humility and sparks the fire,
To rise above, and reach higher and higher.

So let us cherish failure, for it holds the key,
To unlocking our potential, setting ourselves free.
For in the face of failure, we find our true worth,
And realize that failure is but a rebirth.

Failure's Symphony

Failure, a note in life's grand symphony,
Adding depth and richness to our melody.
In every missed beat and off-key tune,
A chance to learn, grow, and opportune.

For failure is not a mark of shame,
But a chapter in a story we proudly claim.
It teaches us resilience and fortitude,
To embrace the challenges with gratitude.

So let us play on, with failure as our guide,
For in its presence, we truly abide.
For failure is not an end, but a beginning anew,
To create a symphony that is uniquely you.

Love's Resurgence

In the depths of sorrow, when hope seemed lost,
Love emerged, like a phoenix from the frost.
For in the aftermath of loss, a seed was sown,
A chance for love to bloom, to be reborn.

With tender hearts, we dared to believe,
That love could heal the wounds and relieve.
And as time passed, the pain began to wane,
Replaced by a love that would forever remain.

In finding love again after loss's sting,
We discovered strength in the joy it would bring.
For love, resilient and steadfast in its might,
Guided us through the darkest of nights.

Love's Renewal

In the wake of loss, when the world felt cold,
Love found a way, its story still untold.
For in the depths of grief, a fire sparked,
A chance to mend the wounds, and love embarked.

With cautious steps, we opened our hearts,
Allowing love to mend the broken parts.
And as we embraced the journey anew,
Love's renewal brought colors back to view.

In finding love again after loss's toll,
We discovered solace in its gentle fold.
For love, like a beacon, guided us through,
A testament to the strength we once thought few.

Love's Redemption

After the storm of loss, we found our way,
Love's redemption leading us astray.
For in the midst of pain, a flicker of light,
A chance to love again, to set things right.

With hesitant hearts, we dared to embrace,
The possibility of love's warm embrace.
And as we let go of the past's heavy weight,
Love's redemption became our ultimate fate.

In finding love again after loss's blow,
We discovered a love that would forever grow.
For love, forgiving and kind in its grace,
Brought healing to the spaces once replaced.

Love's Resilience

In the aftermath of loss, a glimmer of hope,
Love's resilience helping us to cope.
For in the face of darkness, love remained,
A chance for a new chapter to be gained.

With fragile hearts, we took a leap,
Embracing love's embrace, our souls to keep.
And as we allowed love to mend our scars,
Resilience bloomed like a field of stars.

In finding love again after loss's ache,
We discovered the strength that love could make.
For love, unyielding and fierce in its fight,
Brought us back to life, filled with pure delight.

Love's Rebirth

After the ashes of loss, love found its way,
A rebirth of love, a brand new day.
For in the midst of sorrow, love arose,
A chance to heal, to mend what was once closed.

With open hearts, we welcomed love's embrace,
Allowing it to fill the empty space.
And as we embraced love's sweet refrain,
Rebirth unfolded, washing away the pain.

In finding love again after loss's sting,
We discovered the joy that love could bring.
For love, like a phoenix, rose from the fall,
A testament to the power of love above all.

The Light of Friendship

In the darkest of days, when shadows loom,
Friendship emerges, dispelling the gloom.
For in the depths of despair, a hand reaches out,
A beacon of light, erasing all doubt.

Through trials and tribulations, side by side,
Friends stand strong, their bond amplified.
With warmth and understanding, they provide,
A refuge in darkness, a comforting guide.

In the darkest of days, friendship prevails,
A light that never falters, never fails.
For in the embrace of a true friend's care,
Hope is rekindled, burdens become easier to bear.

A Friend's Embrace

When the world feels heavy, and skies turn gray,
A friend's embrace can brighten the way.
For in the depths of despair, a friend's hand,
Offers solace and strength, helping us to stand.

In the midst of darkness, a friend's light shines,
Guiding us through the labyrinth of troubled times.
With empathy and compassion, they understand,
The importance of friendship, a steady hand.

In dark days, when hope feels far away,
A friend's embrace brings comfort, come what may.
For in their presence, we find strength anew,
Friendship's power, forever true.

The Healing Power of Friendship

In the depths of sorrow, when all seems lost,
Friendship's healing power comes at no cost.
For in the midst of pain, a friend's support,
Brings solace and comfort of a different sort.

Through tears and laughter, they stand by our side,
A constant presence, a comforting guide.
With their words and actions, they mend our hearts,
Rekindling hope, igniting fresh starts.

In dark days, when the world feels cold,
Friendship's warmth brings a love untold.
For in their embrace, we find respite,
A reminder that we're not alone in our fight.

E

The Unbreakable Bond of Friendship

In the face of adversity, when skies turn gray,
Friendship stands strong, come what may.
For in the depths of despair, a friend's hand,
Offers unwavering support, helping us to withstand.

Through storms and trials, they remain by our side,
An unbreakable bond, a constant guide.
With their unwavering loyalty and care,
Friendship becomes a sanctuary, always there.

In the darkest of days, when hope seems lost,
Friendship's light shines brightest, no matter the cost.
For in their presence, we find strength anew,
A testament to the power of friendship, tried and true.

The Gift of Friendship

In the midst of darkness, when shadows prevail,
Friendship emerges, like a timeless tale.
For in the depths of despair, a friend's love,
Brings light and warmth, from high above.

Through thick and thin, they walk by our side,
A gift of friendship, a love that won't hide.
With their unwavering support and care,
Friendship becomes a lifeline, beyond compare.

In dark days, when the world feels bleak,
Friendship's presence becomes the strength we seek.
For in their embrace, we find solace and peace,
A reminder that true friendship will never cease.

In a world full of chaos and strife,
I want to express my gratitude in this life.
For your kindness and support, I am grateful,
In my heart, your presence is truly delightful.

Thank you for the smiles you bring,
For the joy and laughter that make my heart sing.
Your words of encouragement uplift my soul,
In your friendship, I find solace and feel whole.

Through ups and downs, you've been there,
A pillar of strength, showing me you care.
Your selflessness and generosity shine bright,
Guiding me through the darkest of nights.

Thank you for the moments we've shared,
For the memories created and the love we've bared.
Your friendship is a treasure I hold dear,
A bond that I cherish, year after year.

In this journey of life, I'm grateful for you,
For the kindness and compassion you always do.
Thank you for being a friend so true,
I'm blessed to have someone like you.

Dadicated to David+ , because you are with me every step oft he way

To my children for you i would do anything and everything
Noah , Lilly and Bo
Love you always
mama